Christian Crackers
Through the Year

365 jokes to lighten your day

Collected by

PHIL MASON

M
BO

First published in the UK in 2005 by Monarch Books
(a publishing imprint of Lion Hudson plc),
Mayfield House, 256 Banbury Road, Oxford, OX2 7DH.
Tel: +44 (0) 1865 302750   Fax: +44 (0) 1865 302757
Email: monarch@lionhudson.com
www.lionhudson.com

ISBN 1 85424 707 7 (UK)
ISBN 0 8254 6086 7 (USA)

Distributed by:
UK: Marston Book Services Ltd, PO Box 269,
Abingdon, Oxon OX14 4YN;
USA: Kregel Publications, PO Box 2607, Grand Rapids,
Michigan 49501.

Unless otherwise stated, Scripture quotations are taken from the
Holy Bible, New International Version, © 1973, 1978, 1984
by the International Bible Society. Used by permission of
Hodder and Stoughton Ltd. All rights reserved.
All remaining quotations are taken from the English Standard Version of the
Bible, published by HarperCollins Publishers,
© 2001 by Crossway Books, a division of Good News Publishers.
Used by permission. All rights reserved.

British Library Cataloguing Data
A catalogue record for this book is available from the British Library.

Printed in Singapore.

1 January

Laughter is like music that
lingers in the heart,
And when its melody is heard,
The ills of life depart.

Remember –

A SMILE ADDS TO YOUR
FAITH'S VALUE

2 January

The rector was preaching about the relationship between "Fact and Faith".

"That you are sitting in front of me in church is Fact," he said. "That I am speaking to you from this pulpit is Fact. But it is only Faith that makes me believe that any of you are listening."

31 December

Self service

A report by *Southwark News* of a visit to Walsingham said: "Afterwards the bishop walked among the crowds eating their picnic lunches."

Overheard in the vestry

"The congregation's a bit thin this morning," said the rector. "Did you tell them I was preaching?"

"No, rector, I didn't," replied the churchwarden. "But you know how things get out."

30 December

Notice outside a church

PRAYER IS THE ONLY COMMODITY THAT IS ALWAYS GOING UP

4 January

There were not many weddings in the West Country village and when it was not in use the verger had the habit of keeping the banns register under the seat cushion of the rector's stall. One Sunday there were some banns to be called and the rector began the familiar "I publish the banns of marriage between…" before he realized that the register was not out ready for him. In his very audible Somerset brogue the verger's voice was heard across the chancel – "Between the cushion and the seat."

29 December

A few years ago a party from church went to sing carols at an old people's home in the parish. After we had sung several well-known carols, I asked the residents, "Is there anything you would like?" One elderly lady replied, "I would like to go to bed."

5 January

From Scotland

Having preached for half an hour the minister asked, "And what shall I say more?"

A voice replied, "Say Amen, mon, and sit doon."

The minister visited a patient in hospital who was recovering from a very serious operation. He was met by the words: "I vaguely remember you coming yesterday and thinking 'I can't be in heaven because there is the minister'."

6 January

At a crowded church meeting the rector asked: "Can you hear me at the back?"

A voice at the back said, "Yes, I can hear you perfectly well but I don't mind changing with somebody who can't."

27 December

From the bulletin

At our June meeting Mrs May Johnson, who has been a faithful member for many years, celebrated her 80th birthday. Her son-in-law Mr Richard Stokes spoke about "God's Weeds".

7 January

The new rector had preached his first sermon but a sudden emergency had prevented one of the churchwardens from attending church that day. When the churchwarden saw the rector during the week, the following conversation took place.

Churchwarden: "I was so sorry to have missed you first sermon, rector."

Rector (with great modesty): "Oh, you didn't miss much."

Churchwarden: "So they tell me."

26 December

A friend's little girl was sitting in church with my daughter. We usually have the offering early in the service, but this particular morning the order of service had been changed and the offering was coming later. In a loud voice during a prayer the little girl said, "When are the men coming for the fares?"

8 January

A minister coming home from church one Sunday met two little boys proudly carrying fishing nets and jars full of tiddlers. "Do you know where little boys go who go fishing on Sunday?" he said solemnly.

"Oh yes," one of them replied eagerly, "up the cut and under the third bridge."

Christmas spirit

After a glass or two of sherry, the teacher on duty rushed through to the dining room to say grace before the Christmas dinner. His order to the whole school: "Eyes together and hands closed".

9 January

My cousin, a Methodist minister, was arranging a wedding service for a widower who was remarrying. One of the hymns he requested was "My God, I thank thee who hast made the earth so bright" which contains the verse:

I thank thee Lord, that thou hast
    kept the best in store;
We have enough, yet not too much
    to long for more –
A yearning for a deeper peace not
    known before.

A Methodist minister at the September Synod was asked to attend a meeting the following June. Looking in his diary he said, "I'm sorry, I can't go, I have two funerals that week."

The theme of a Sunday morning sermon by a Glasgow minister was that "every blade of grass held a sermon". The next day he was mowing his lawn when a passing parishioner said, "That's the ticket, minister – keep 'em short."

Minister, addressing children in church: "Can anyone tell me who is the Perfect Person to whom I must compare my life?"

Child (hesitantly): "Is it your wife?"

11 January

My mother had an aunt of mine staying with her. One day they visited our local parish church and Auntie wanted to sign the visitors' book. There was no book in evidence but a list containing names and addresses, so they signed that. All was well until the rector called for the deposits for a trip to Oberammergau. Fortunately my mother attended the daughter church and was known to him.

Only temporary residence

I was taking the service at a local Baptist church when the choir left the gallery to come and sit in front of me for the sermon. They did this during the last verse of "Love divine" and as they were singing: "Now we cast our crowns before thee till in heaven we take our place".

12 January

Sound advice

Wife to minister as he left for a meeting: "Drive carefully, my dear. Remember it's not only a car that can be recalled by its maker."

21 December

Seen in a parish magazine

We are all in favour of change as long as it doesn't make any difference.

13 January

The rector told the congregation that he would shortly be leaving to move to another parish. However he assured them that the bishop had promised to send a good man to take over. After the service he noticed a woman crying and said, "Don't get upset, my dear, the bishop has promised to send a good man to take over."

"He told us that the last time," replied the woman in tears.

God made the world,
then He rested.
He then made man
and rested again.
He then made
woman, since when,
nothing has rested.

14 January

The rector was ill in hospital and was visited by his churchwarden who said, "Rector, we had a meeting of the Parochial Church Council last night and a resolution put forward wishing you a speedy recovery was passed by fourteen votes to twelve."

19 December

A rector leaving his parish to take up a new appointment as a prison chaplain, used as the text for his final sermon in the parish:

I go to prepare a place for you

A priest was a Doctor of Divinity and his wife was a Doctor of Medicine. A man called at the rectory and asked if he could see "the Doctor". The housekeeper took one look at him and said, "Which one do you want ... the preaching one or the practising one?"

18 December

The secretary of a village church received a letter from the television licence office addressed to "The Present Occupier" of the church, asking why there was no record of a TV licence. The secretary replied,

"The present occupier is God. He took up residence in 1876 when his house was opened and consecrated. As he is an all-seeing God he has no need for a television set."

16 January

In the 1950s Her Majesty Queen Elizabeth, the Queen Mother, visited the Church of Scotland in Dumfries. As she was walking through the graveyard after the service, she asked the Lord Provost, "Why are the headstones so large?"

He replied, "To hold them doon, Ma'am."

17 December

A member of the congregation saw an elderly chapel steward take money off the plate before taking up the collection. After the service he remarked kindly about this to him. The steward brought a £5 note from his pocket and said:

"This £5 note has started the collection for the past ten years."

17 January

At the end of the rector's pre-Lent sermon he suggested, as an example to the rest of the community, the congregation should worship in an unheated church for the whole of Lent. As they made their way out into the chill Sunday air the rector addressed one member of the congregation asking what she had decided to give up for Lent.

...ARE YOU SURE **YOU** SHOULD GIVE UP GOING TO CHURCH FOR LENT?!

"Church," she replied firmly.

Seen on a church door

THIS IS THE GATE OF HEAVEN ENTER YE ALL BY THIS DOOR

Underneath someone had written:

THIS DOOR IS KEPT LOCKED BECAUSE OF THE DRAUGHT. PLEASE USE THE OTHER ENTRANCE.

18 January

"At this point I should be saying a prayer for the blessing of the water," said a priest in Woking. "Unfortunately it's all gone down the plughole."

15 December

An elderly couple died and were received by St Peter through the Pearly Gates into heaven. After a while they found it a wonderful place. The husband said to his wife, "If you hadn't have come up with all those healthy foods we could have been here years ago."

19 January

The donkey failed to arrive for the Palm Sunday procession at St Peter's Church, Chippenham. The procession was led by the rector, the Revd Jeremy Bray.

14 December

Seen in a parish bulletin

There will be a procession in the grounds of the monastery next Sunday afternoon. If it rains in the afternoon the procession will take place in the morning.

20 January

One Sunday I was on sidesman's duty at our Methodist church. We had a christening with a crowd of relatives. Just as the first hymn started two strangers came in. I approached with hymn books and said, "Are you with the christening party?"

The man immediately replied, "No, I'm with the Woolwich."

13 December

The theme of St James Church Flower Festival was: "Enter not into temptation". As visitors followed the programme around the church they came upon two stark arrangements of driftwood and dried seed heads entitled: "Hunger" and "Thirst". On the wall close by was a large notice:

REFRESHMENTS IN THE CHURCH ROOM

Some years ago we held a children's service at 6.00 p.m. as well as the main evening service at 6.30 p.m. The teachers, joining the congregation at the main service during the hymn before the sermon, entered the gallery by way of a high staircase behind the organ. One Sunday evening they appeared just as the congregation started to sing the hymn, "Come sinners to the Gospel Feast".

12 December

The service sheet from a church visited whilst on holiday read:

PLEASE NOTE: From next Sunday the Evening Service will be at 8 p.m.

This will continue until the 13th September.

22 January

The Presbyterian Church in Ireland brought out a new hymn book. In the first print a hymn for funerals was unfortunately included in the marriage section.

The hymn was "Go, happy soul, thy days are ended."

From the forthcoming events column of a Birmingham parish newsletter: "Pram service in church, followed by talk about the wind."

23 January

Some years ago a bishop of St David's on holiday in a Welsh village was asked to conduct the Sunday worship as the rector was ill. Commented the rector's warden, "A worser preacher would have done but we couldn't find one."

A report on renovations at a youth centre in Northants: "The lift and the new windows are installed and the non-alcoholic bar is already plastered."

24 January

A baptismal service was in progress at our local Anglican church. During the course of his sermon the minister looked down at the water in the font and said, "There is nothing magical about this water, it is the same water that we shall use to make the coffee with later."

9 December

The service sheet read:

Hymns: MP 163   Now thank we all
our God

MP 222   The king is among us
(If required)

25 January

Seen in a paper in India

Sacred to the memory of Revd Pugh who, after twenty years of unremitting labour as a missionary, was accidentally shot by his native bearer.

"WELL DONE THOU GOOD AND FAITHFUL SERVANT"

8 December

Seen in the *Cumberland Times*

A man accused of stealing candlesticks from Carlisle Cathedral had his case temporarily adjourned when the court heard he had wax in his ears.

26 January

The rector, passing an elderly gentleman attending to his garden, remarked,

"How wonderful you and God have made your garden, Harry."

"Yes, rector," said Harry, "but you should have seen it when God had it on his own."

From London

One Sunday morning it was noted that the office bearers counting the offertory were Messrs Robb, Crook and Cheatham.

27 January

Minister's wife as husband set off to conduct a funeral in a cemetery:

"Now don't go standing with your bare head on that damp ground."

6 December

From an advertisement in the
Huddersfield Examiner

"H reg. Nissan Micra in red, one Reverend owner from new, never missed a service."

The bishop consulted his doctor who said,

"You must winter on the Riviera."

"Out of the question," declared the bishop, "I have far too much work to do."

The doctor said, "It's either the Riviera or heaven."

"Dear, dear," said the bishop. "It must be the Riviera then."

"It was agreed that Mr Mellor be asked to patch up the footpath in Church Street, between the rectory and the George and Dragon."

P.C.C. minute, quoted in the *Daily Telegraph*

29 January

A middle-aged couple were married during the week. After the wedding the groom asked the minister, "How much do I owe you?" The minister said, "How much is she worth?" The groom gave the minister £1. The minister took a second look at the bride and gave him 50p back.

4 December

An American bishop, after staying at a hotel, had an extortionate bill presented to him. After he had paid he was asked if he had enjoyed the change and the rest. "No, I have had neither," replied the bishop, "the waiter had the change, and you've had the rest."

30 January

From the Notices

ORGANIST REQUIRED … Small but trying priest and congregation.

From Canada

A bishop attended one of his remoter parishes. As he walked down the aisle he noticed just five people present and asked the rector, "Did you tell the people I was coming?"

"No," replied the rector, "but heaven help the person who did."

31 January

Heard on the local radio

The Nether Heyford Baptist Ladies have a chiropodist to speak at their meeting next week. No doubt his text will be: "Blessed are the feet that wait upon the Lord."

One minister, giving advice to the young couple, said to the groom, "Tonight you'll sink in her arms, tomorrow you'll have your arms in her sink."

1 February

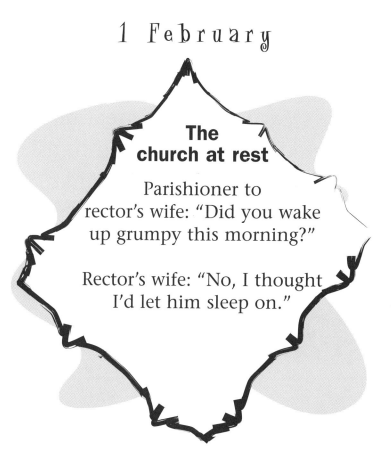

The church at rest

Parishioner to rector's wife: "Did you wake up grumpy this morning?"

Rector's wife: "No, I thought I'd let him sleep on."

1 December

A young bride, anxious about the weather for the great day, phoned the weatherman to ask what it was going to be like. She received the answer –

Warm and close with a little son later

2 February

A man was collecting Christian Aid envelopes. Calling at one house he met the response, "Sorry I can't give you anything, the dog ate the envelope."

"Ah," said the collector. "Don't worry, I have a spare envelope." Back came the quick reply, "It's no good, he'd only eat that one too."

From this day forward

Minister to groom:
"Wilt thou take this woman to
be thy lawful wedded wife?"
Groom, looking at bride:
"I wilt."

3 February

The last word

As a member of any church committee will tell you:

After all is said and done, there's a lot more said than done.

Seen on a church notice board in Manchester

WE OFFER SOULING
AND HEALING
SERVICES
STEP INSIDE

A father, who was a minister, had been sitting watching the second hand of a new electric clock. "It's amazing how long it takes for that hand to move round one minute," he said.

"I'm glad you've noticed that, Dad," said his son. "Now you know what it's like to sit through 35 of them."

28 November

From Canada

Every year in the Diocese of Huron we have a children's festival which gathers around 1,200 children. Each year something funny happens including the following. A young native American child told his rector on returning from the festival, "We had a clown there with a pointed hat."

5 February

A large car pulled up outside a village church. The elderly verger was busy mowing the grass. The window slid down and a voice with a strong American accent said, "Say, any great men born around these parts?"

"Nope," came the reply, "only babies."

27 November

Whilst the message on another notice board read:

Have you a long standing problem?
Try kneeling

The minister was being carried away by his own exuberance in leading prayers. He began, "O thou who rulest the raging of the sea, the fierceness of the winds …" Then he seemed to lose himself for a moment, but soon carried on – "Bless our wives."

26 November

Seen on a church notice board

COME IN FOR A FAITH LIFT

Keep smiling, it makes the world a happier place.

25 November

From Southampton's Spring Road Evangelical Church bulletin

The congregation was truly cosmopolitan with guests coming from as far away as Australia and some from Barrow-in-Furness.

8 February

A man's favourite method of receiving guidance was to open his bible and pick out random verses. One day he opened his bible and read:

So Judas went out and hanged himself.

Feeling a little puzzled he opened his bible again and read:

Go and do thou likewise.

Still needing reassurance he opened his bible a third time and saw:

Whatever you do, do it quickly.

24 November

**Seen on a church notice board
in Northampton**

**SATURDAY CLUB
NO MEETING ON EASTER
MONDAY**

9 February

After an organ overhaul, the organ builder left a note for the lady organist as follows: "You will now be able to change your combinations without taking your feet off the pedals."

23 November

**From the news sheet
of St James' Church, Gatley**

*Tuesday – Pancakes at the Vicarage –
cancelled due to dry
rot.*

10 February

A Sunday School teacher was telling how Lot's wife looked back and was turned into a pillar of salt. "That's nothing," said one boy. "My mother was driving the car the other day and she looked back and turned into a telegraph pole."

From the bulletin of St George's Church, Tolworth

Hymn 543
Shine Jesus shine
(on the overhead
projector)

11 February

A minister commenting about the shortage of qualified organists said that although the organist did her best to struggle through the hymns, his long-suffering congregation still had to play *Name That Tune In Ten* at the beginning of each hymn.

21 November

From the notices

From the parish of Warwick newsletter

Monday 7.30 p.m. Holy Communion. There will be no "time to pray" today.

Daily Telegraph

12 February

During a church service a little girl had to go outside because she didn't feel very well. She returned a few minutes later and admitted, "I have been a little sick but it doesn't matter, there's a box at the door marked 'For the Sick'."

Believe it or not

The wedding music chosen by two young vegetarians included the voluntary "Sheep may safely graze".

13 February

In the good old days the parishes in east London used to get the schoolchildren to church on Ascension Day and then take them off for an outing. The popular place for All Saints, Poplar was Chessington Zoo. When 5 p.m. came there was a great gathering-up operation by rectors, curates and sisters on the large green. A loud voice called across the green to our lot boarding the coach, "Are you Holy Innocents?" and the shout went back, "No, we're all SAINTS."

19 November

The minister had travelled from Birmingham to London to attend to the details of a new banner that was being made for his church. On his arrival he discovered that he had lost the piece of paper with the details on. He sent his wife a telegram asking her to send details by return. When the answer arrived at the post office, the postmistress almost fainted when she read:

"UNTO US A CHILD IS BORN. EIGHT FEET LONG. THREE FEET WIDE. ASSORTED COLOURS."

14 February

Whilst on holiday one year my brother and I attended the local church. On the way my brother had a fall, which delayed us somewhat. We entered as the congregation was singing the first hymn:

"Courage, brother, do not stumble"

18 November

Seen in a church magazine

If any readers have either a single bed or a man's bicycle to enable the rector to get around his scattered parish, Mr Jones would be pleased to collect them.

15 February

Some years ago the canon at a Sheffield church used to like not only to attend all the parish groups, but also to identify himself with them by belonging to them, so that he could address them as "We Rover Scouts" or "We Catholic Teachers". One day he went too far and began, "We Catholic Mothers".

A former rector used to memorize the telephone numbers of his parishioners by the first line of the corresponding number in *Hymns Ancient and Modern*. Was it just coincidence that the telephone number of the local postmaster (whose family were all much involved in church activities) was 215 – "The church's one foundation", and that of the doctor was 225 – "Brief life is here our portion"?

Some advice to preachers

If after ten minutes you don't strike oil – THEN STOP BORING.

16 November

True stories

In the early 1950s my grandmother was Communion steward at Thurscoe East in South Yorkshire. There was to be an early Communion Service on Christmas morning, so she went to the chapel on Christmas Eve to prepare the bread and wine. When the minister lifted off the cloth during the service, he discovered that the mice had eaten the bread.

17 February

Our minister, on entering the church and finding water on the floor (due to burst pipes), said later, "So I went into the church and mopped the floor with my wife."

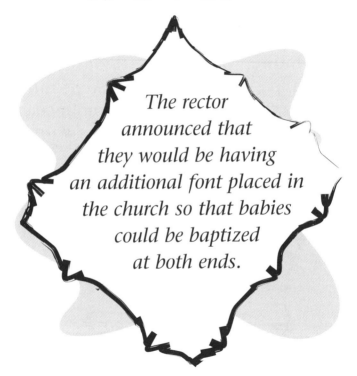

15 November

The rector
announced that
they would be having
an additional font placed in
the church so that babies
could be baptized
at both ends.

18 February

A Yorkshireman wanted an inscription on his wife's gravestone to read – "She was Thine". The engraver mistakenly put "She was Thin". The man wrote back saying they had missed out the "E". The next effort read: " 'E' She was Thin".

14 November

From the notices

"We regret to announce that the 'Ladies Happy Hour' are heavily in debt following their recent **'Sponsored silence'**."

19 February

The preacher in the Dome at Brighton had just given out his text: "Paul we know, and Apollos we know, but who are these?"

The stewards were just showing in two latecomers. One called out: "They are two businessmen staying at the Queen's Hotel."

13 November

From Wales

A young lad was taken by his father to hear a visiting clergyman give a talk. The speaker, a large hefty man, started off by saying, "I am a self-made man and proud of it." Later, when all was quiet, a voice was heard to say: "Daddy, if he made himself why did he make his nose so big and crooked?"

20 February

It is said that Archbishop Tench of Dublin in his latter years had a fear of sudden crippling paralysis. At a dinner on one occasion he suddenly said, "It's come at last, total lack of feeling in my right leg." A woman sitting next to him said, "Your Grace, it may be of some comfort and relief for you to know that during the whole of this meal it is my leg that you have been pinching."

From Canada

The parish newspaper of St Luke's Anglican Church, London, Ontario welcomed the arrival of an Ethiopian refugee, Halleluiah Ayenew, to the parish. The first Sunday Halleluiah attended St Luke's, the choir's anthem without premeditation was "Alleluia he is coming, Alleluia he is here".

21 February

The *Fleet and District Courier* carried an advertisement for a "full-time bar parson" to work in Heath End.

Presumably only spirit-filled clergy need apply.

11 November

From Australia

A newspaper report of a local wedding said, "The bride looked stunning in an embroidered gown which fell softly to the floor."

An elderly Irishman who was dying was visited by his priest.

"Will you renounce the devil and all his works?" asked the priest. There was no answer.

The priest shouted, "Murphy, will you renounce the devil and all his works?"

The old man opened one eye and said, "You needn't shout Father, I heard you the first time, but this is no time to be making enemies."

10 November

After a bishop had heard himself introduced over-flatteringly, he said he had just sent up two prayers – one for the man who had told so many lies, and the other for himself for enjoying it so much.

23 February

A new rector was inducted into a country parish. One of the older parishioners was asked how he liked the new rector and he replied, "Well, it's like this, the old rector when he said 'and in conclusion' he concluded. This new rector when he says 'and lastly' he lasts."

9 November

An Irish bishop tells how some people get nervous when they have to call him "My Lord". On one occasion a woman was serving him a cup of tea when she picked up the sugar bowl and said, "How many Lords, my lump?"

24 February

From a parish magazine

Burial of the dead held over to next month owing to lack of space.

True story

It was our harvest festival Sunday. My husband had cut his ear while shaving. We arrived at the church to sing – "First the blade and then the ear".

25 February

A church magazine in Berkshire advertised

Car engine for sale by curate slightly cracked.

From Cornwall

There was a well-known Methodist "local preacher" who was very short. One Sunday morning he was preaching at Helston Wesley Chapel, and because the pulpit was so high he stood on an orange box. He announced, "My text is, 'A little while you see me and in a little while you will see me not'." Just at that point the orange box gave way and he disappeared from sight.

The young rector had spent all his life in towns and didn't really understand his rural parishioners. Deploring a townsman's ignorance, a farm worker said, "He knows no more 'bout farmin' than a cow 'bout Sunday."

Seen on a tombstone

Whoe'er you are, as you pass by
As you are now so once was I,
As I am now sometime you'll be,
Prepare yourself to follow me.

Underneath someone had written:

To follow thee we've no intent,
Until we know the way thee went.

27 February

True story

In the days of compulsory church parades, a sergeant major marched the men to the Garrison Anglican Church, then became muddled as he announced, "Roam out the fallen Catholics."

5 November

An Irish priest was visiting Niagara Falls with his friend, an Irish plumber. "Just look at that, Patrick," he said in wonder.

"Sure, Father," came the reply, "I can fix it."

28 February

The rector was praying for the sick and said, "We must remember Mrs Godson in our prayers who has recently had all her teeth taken out and a new gas stove put in."

Father came home from work to find his small son busily drawing. "What picture are you drawing?" he asked.

"God," said the little fellow while his father looked on smiling. "You can't draw God," he said, "No one knows what he looks like." "They will soon," came the reply, "I've nearly finished."

Seen on a tombstone

August 7th 1714
Mary, the wife of Joseph Yates,
of Lizard Common
was buried aged 127.
She walked to London just
after the fire in 1666,
was hearty and strong
at 120 years,
and married a third husband
at 92.

3 November

My son, Douglas, aged three, was brought up to the altar rail for a blessing while his mother received Communion. When the bread was passed he opened his mouth like a little bird and gave me an angry look when I passed him by. When I passed him by with the wine also, he held his peace until I was down the line and then shouted, "Hey, Daddy, I want some beer too."

2 March

Whilst sitting at a table in a public restaurant a lady was joined by two nuns. Out of curiosity she enquired of them, "What is your order?" (meaning religious community). The nuns replied, "Sausage and chips."

CONVENT

SACRED
ORDER
OF THE
PERPETUAL
MENU

2 November

Wilson Huff was a handsome stoney-faced native American who looked like the picture on the U.S. five cent piece. I once suggested that we buy new pews. "Reverend Murray wanted to do that once," he said.

"What happened?" I ventured.

"I told him that my grandfather had made these pews and that it was easier to get a new minister than new pews."

3 March

Misprint

The newsletter at All Saints Church, Margaret Street, London reminds the congregation that "Hot Smacks" are available after the Mass.

From Canada

A bishop visiting a parish once made the comment: "This tea tastes like water," not realizing that the lady who made the tea was serving him. She retorted: "My Lord, when I make tea, I make tea, and when I make water, I make water."

4 March

Shortly after attending the funeral, two old men were discussing the will of their deceased friend. "What did he leave?" asked one. "Everything," replied the other.

**From
the church
bulletin**

MORE SINNERS
WANTED FOR
THE CHOIR

5 March

The family service was being conducted by a visiting clergyman during the rector's absence. He asked the children what they were giving up for Lent.

Quick as a flash, one little toddler answered: "The rector."

Seen on a church notice board

VISITORS WELCOME
MEMBERS EXPECTED

6 March

An elderly rector idolized children and during baptism was wont to put his face close to them and smile at them. One Sunday however, the infant was older (and sharper) than usual. Making good its opportunity, it plunged its fist into the rector's mouth and withdrew it with a triumphant handful of teeth.

29 October

From a church magazine

We shall be meeting on Wednesday 11th April when the subject will be: "Heaven. How do we get there?" Transport is available at 7.55 p.m. from the bus stop opposite the Harewood Arms.

Daily Telegraph

7 March

The rector had been unwell and a parishioner asked his housekeeper how he was. She replied, "It's his head you know, it's been on and off all the week."

From Canada

A minister in British Columbia had not had a rehearsal with the couple and so whispered instructions to them all through the wedding ceremony. When the time came for them to proceed to the chancel rail for the blessing, he leaned over and whispered, "Follow me!" When he turned to find out what the laughter was all about, he saw that the couple were indeed following him – still kneeling.

8 March

The rector of the Good Shepherd parish in the diocese of Texas, whilst asking his congregation to pray on one occasion added,
"I bid you also to pray for those who are **sick of this parish**."

Sleep walking?

When a man walked out during the sermon, his wife made the excuse that he was apt to walk in his sleep.

9 March

During his notices the rector announced, "Members of the Mothers' Union and Young Wives' Group will be attending Evensong next Sunday. The choir will sing the anthem 'What Are These?' "

26 October

True story

During my years as a minister's wife, I did a lot of visiting. At one house the old woman was very fond of her gramophone, the old-fashioned kind which her granddaughter had to wind up when it ran down. The thing was always on, usually playing some lively music, but if I called, the old woman would answer the door and shout, "Kathleen, put that off and put 'Lead kindly light' on – the minister's wife is here."

When a Devonshire rector had faithfully served his parish for 60 years he received a letter of congratulation from his bishop with the tactful suggestion that he might now like to think of retirement.

The rector replied that when he was instituted in 1888 he was given to understand that it was not a temporary appointment.

Advert for someone to help with the church magazine:

Must have own computer and a sense of humour.

11 March

When Dr Robert Runcie, former Archbishop of Canterbury, was in the U.S.A., an American said to him, "You sound like an Englishman."

"I am," he replied.

"Did you see the royal wedding?" the American asked.

"Yes," the Archbishop answered, "in fact I had a very good view."

"Gee," said the American. "You must have got there early."

24 October

A reader visiting Cumbria went to an organ recital and was intrigued to hear that details of further musical events could be found on the CHURCHWARDENS' CHEST.

Church Times

A clergyman was driving his sports car at a fast pace. He had to scream to a standstill to avoid an accident. When the angry driver of the other car stormed over to exchange words, the rector handed him his card –

The Revd Paul Brown is sorry
to have missed you.
He hopes to make contact
with you next time.

23 October

One day Pope John XXIII visited the hospital of the Holy Spirit in Rome, which is administered by a religious sisterhood. Deeply moved by the Papal visitation, the Mother Superior introduced herself. "Most Holy Father, I am the Superior of the Holy Spirit."

"Well, I must say you are fortunate," replied the Pope. "I am only the Vicar of Christ."

13 March

Members of an Anglican
church discovered that
the roof was leaking.
The following
Sunday the
church secretary
started his
notices by
apologizing for
**the drip in the
pulpit**.

22 October

The Sunday notices reported that:

The **Standing Committee** had sat for three hours.

14 March

While a male choir in St Mawgan, Cornwall, was singing "When the stars begin to fall", part of the large pulpit on which the choir stood gave way, and the baritones and second tenors fell through. No one was hurt, and within five minutes they were back in action with "My anchor holds".

Oxford Mail

21 October

The minister slipped and fell. He was confronted by a small girl who said, "Let me help you up, mister."

The minister said: "That's kind of you but I can manage and you are rather small."

"No trouble," she replied. "I've helped my father up when he was far drunker than you are."

QUICK - GET UP BEFORE THEY COME AND BREATHALYSE YOU!

15 March

A bookseller wrote to a Chicago firm for a dozen copies of Dean Farrar's *Seekers after God*. He received a telegram in reply which read: "No seekers after God in Chicago, try Philadelphia"!

20 October

A new Sunday School teacher had succeeded one who always told a story and then went on to say: "And the moral of the story is … " When the minister asked a boy how he liked the new teacher, he got the reply: "Oh Miss … is great, she hasn't got any morals."

16 March

"I don't want to go to church this morning!" said the son to his mother. "The people don't like me, they talk behind my back and the service is too long."

"But you have to go," came the reply. "You're the rector."

The poet Dryden wrote
this epitaph for his wife.

Here lies my wife.
Here let her lie.
Now she's at rest.
And so am I.

17 March

A musical concert was about to be performed in a prison. The governor was talking to a titled lady explaining that the orchestra was made up of murderers, embezzlers and other hardened criminals. The lady pointed to a man holding a trombone and said, "He looks a tough customer." The governor smiled and said, "I ought to explain my dear, he is the chaplain."

18 October

Seen on a tombstone in Edinburgh

Erected to the
memory of
John MacFarlane
Drowned in the
waters of Leith
By a few affectionate
friends.

When a rector had been in his new parish twelve months a parishioner asked him what he thought had been his main contribution to the life of the church. He replied, "People here didn't know what sin was till I came."

17 October

Grave situations

A minister was asked to take a funeral at short notice. At one point in the service he said, "As I did not know the deceased, is there anyone here who would like to say a few words of tribute?" There was silence for a while, then a voice at the back was heard to say: "His brother was far worse."

The rector announced, "After the blessing the bishop will leave and we shall sing 'Now thank we all our God'."

16 October

Three boys were bragging about the jobs their fathers had.

"My dad scribbles a few words on a piece of paper, calls it poetry and people give him £50 for it," said the first.

"That's nothing," said the second boy. "My dad scribbles a few words on a piece of paper, calls it a song and gets £100."

"I can do better than both of you," smiled the third boy. "My dad scribbles a few words on a piece of paper, calls it a sermon, and it takes six people to collect the money."

20 March

"I hope you will be happy," said the minister to the newly married couple.

"I don't see why not," said the bridegroom. "I came through the war all right."

A churchwarden complained to the bishop that the new curate wore a hood like an Oxford MA which he was not. "The man has a lie on his back," said the angry churchwarden. "Don't say a lie, Mr Brown," replied the bishop. "Say a false hood!"

21 March

The day after our wedding we were staying in Somerset on our honeymoon where we attended church. The service started earlier than we had been informed and as we entered the church with faces red at being late, the rector announced the hymn "My Father for another night of quiet sleep and rest."

14 October

There are two types of people in the world:

Those who wake up in the morning and say: "Good morning, Lord."

And those who wake up and say: "Good Lord, it's morning."

22 March

The bishop had come to dedicate a new sophisticated public address system. Being unsure as to whether the microphone had been switched on or not, he tapped it gently with seemingly no result. So, leaning very close to the microphone, he said in a loud whisper which echoed around the church,

"THERE IS SOMETHING WRONG WITH THIS MICROPHONE."

The well-trained and responsive congregation, well established in the latest A.S.B. service, replied:

"AND ALSO WITH YOU."

13 October

The *Church Times* reports of a jolly diocesan Mothers Union service, at which the congregation were instructed to stand tall, like stalks of corn, and wave in the breeze. On the draft service sheet was the rubric: **"Congregation to make wind noises."**

Wanted

A woman advertised for a travelling companion, concluding with the words: "Christian wanted, cheerful if possible."

A clergyman phoned his bishop saying, "I am sorry to have to inform you that my wife has died. Could you please send me a substitute for the weekend?"

24 March

From the U.S.A.

Seen on a church bulletin:

Don't let worry kill you – let the church help.

The Anglican Digest

11 October

The young curate was looking after his baby daughter while his wife went shopping. He decided to go fishing and take the toddler along with him. When he returned home he told his wife, "I'll never take her with me again. I didn't catch a thing." His wife said, "Oh next time I'm sure she'll be quiet and not scare the fish away."

"It wasn't that," the father replied. "She ate all the bait."

At the end of his sermon the minister told his congregation that Jesus had called him to another church. The congregation then sang "What a friend we have in Jesus".

10 October

An elderly clergyman just managed to get the train as it was leaving his local station. He jumped in and sat down next to a young girl. When he recovered his breath he realised that he was sitting on her newspaper. He gave it to her. She thanked him but kept looking at him somewhat anxiously. At the next station she prepared to get out and said: "Please sir, may I have my fish too?"

I WONDER IF I MIGHT TROUBLE YOU FOR THE PIECE OF COD?

26 March

Our minister says, "Bibles which are falling apart are read by people who aren't."

9 October

The doctor and the rector were standing at the bedside of an old man who was dying.

"I'm afraid he's gone," said the rector.

"Yes, he has," said the doctor.

"No, I b'aint," murmured the patient, feebly sitting up.

"Lie down, dear," said the wife, "doctor and rector do know best."

27 March

A rather pompous rector asked his confirmation class, "Why do people call me a Christian?"

After some hesitation one lad replied, "Perhaps it's because they don't know you."

8 October

Our minister says

My wife is a very systematic woman. She works on the theory that you can find whatever you want when you don't want it by looking where it wouldn't be if you did want it.

28 March

A parishioner who was rather fond of drink came out of the Red Lion and ran smack into the Rector.

Rector: "Hello, John, you know drink is your greatest enemy."

John: "Yes, Rector, but you always tell us to love our enemies."

Rector: "Ah yes, but I didn't tell you to swallow them."

7 October

From Canada

During Evensong, just as the rector had finished his sermon, all the lights went out for a few seconds. When they came on again he announced the next hymn:

Number 93 – The people that in darkness sat.

Seen on a notice board

6 October

An elderly clergyman muttered and mumbled his way through the services much to the dismay of the congregation who couldn't understand what he was saying. Eventually the churchwardens persuaded him to let lay people read the lessons and say the prayers. He agreed on condition that they spoke clearly and distinctly.

30 March

During an Ash Wednesday service we were heartily singing "Forty days and forty nights" when the church cat appeared marching down the chancel with a pigeon grasped between her teeth. The line we were singing was:

Prowling beasts about thy way ...

5 October

From the order of service for the Mothers' Union family service at Guildford Cathedral:

**"Song 137 –
Let there be love –
Please turn over."**

31 March

I was once at a Scout camp where the service was taken by a bishop. It was a very hot humid summer day and the moderator of the Free Church Federal Council had turned up in his full robes. Standing around sweating buckets and getting hotter and hotter under the dog collar, he turned to our minister and bellowed, "When is that flipping bishop going to turn up?"

A man standing by in his Scouts uniform said, "I'm already here."

When a church in Manchester closed its doors for the last time the denominational magazine informed readers that this had become necessary because of **"swindling congregations"**.

1 April

The Trout Inn, which lies between the villages of Wansford and Driffield at the foot of the Yorkshire Wolds, is a popular port of call for cyclists and ramblers. The elderly vicar of Wansford asked the innkeeper if he would display a notice giving details of the services at the village church. The innkeeper gladly obliged and the notice read:

We will be glad to see you at any of our services
Clothes don't matter

3 October

Rector at Baptism: "Why do you name the child after me? Are you going to make a parson of him?"

"No," replied the father. "He'll have to work for his living."

2 April

To oblige a customer who wanted the *Church Times* the newsagent searched through a pile of papers only to report, "I'm sorry, it hasn't come yet. Several other comics are also late."

2 October

A rather pompous bachelor clergyman, rebuking his housekeeper for using his bath while he was away, said, "I am grieved that you would do behind my back what you would not do in front of my face."

THE BATH TO BE USED ONLY WHEN THE VICAR IS PRESENT!

3 April

A young curate was visiting an elderly man on his 99th birthday to interview him about his long life. The interview over, the curate said: "I hope to see you again on your 100th birthday." The old gentleman carefully looked him over and said: "I can't see any reason why you shouldn't, young man, you look healthy enough to me."

The preacher introduced his sermon with these words: "Now before I start I want to say something."

A Baptist minister complaining about traffic noise in Harpenden is reported as saying: "Sometimes when we have something on in church all hell is let loose."

True story

I teach in our Sunday School and always try to make myself look as attractive as possible. During a particular lesson I put on a face which should have been showing unhappiness. I said to my class, "Tell me – how do I look?"

"Dreadful," said one little girl.

"No, try again," I said.

"**Ugly**," she said.

5 April

A north-country choirmaster was rehearsing the hymns for Sunday, telling the choir the hymns they were to sing, and the tunes to which they were to sing them. He said, "Now then, 'Come ye that love the Lord' to Southport!" A voice called out, "Where are you tekking t'rest of us?"

Small boy to his father during an over-long sermon:

"Daddy, if we give him the money now, do you suppose he will let us go home?"

6 April

"Come, come, this will never do," said the choirmaster, "open your mouths and sing boldly ... 'LITTLE DROPS OF WATER', and for goodness' sake ... put some spirit into it."

Seen on the notice board

SEVEN DAYS
WITHOUT PRAYER
MAKES ONE WEAK

7 April

The rector wrote in his parish magazine

We have been most fortunate this year with our choirmaster and organist. Both have been given appointments that will take them from us.

27 September

A very small girl attended Family Communion for the first time. Telling her father about it afterwards she said: "Everyone went for something to eat, and then they came back and went to sleep."

8 April

Our choir sometimes visits hospitals etc. to give concerts. At one old people's home the organist announced that she would play "Handel's Largo". An old woman sitting close by in a wheelchair said in a loud voice, "Oh, I love a drop of lager."

26 September

A former Bishop of Norwich, Rt Reverend Peter Nott soon got to grips with the Norfolk way of keeping things in perspective.

"I was taking a Communion service in a freezing church in West Norfolk. When it was over I walked to the back of the church. My hands were numb with cold and I had great difficulty grasping the mug of hot coffee the churchwarden gave me. "My goodness, your church is cold," I said.

"Oh yes, Bishop, that is cold," said the churchwarden, "but you should be here when we don't have the heating on."

9 April

We are music teachers and were teaching the nuns at the local convent guitar accompaniment to their choruses. A great favourite was "Alleluia". Without thinking I said, "The first two syllables are unaccompanied – you come in on the LU ..."

25 September

A distinguished clergyman billed to preach at St Mary's Church, Oxford was unable to come owing to ill health and his place was taken by an unknown young man. After entering the pulpit he announced his text:

Art thou he that should come, or look we for another?

10 April

It was the rector's last Sunday and he innocently chose as his final hymn "On our way rejoicing". This was immediately followed by the organist playing as his concluding voluntary "Now thank we all our God".

24 September

The minister announced: "Now that Sister Christine has successfully completed her examinations we want to congratulate her. Will you please remember to pray for all the patients on Ward 3D where she will be working?"

I was attending a relative's wedding together with my son, daughter-in-law and little granddaughter aged two. My daughter-in-law took a bag of jelly babies so that if the little girl became restless she could give her one. During his talk the minister was explaining about marriage and the creation of families when my granddaughter, having just finished her sweet, shouted loudly, "MORE BABIES".

23 September

A friend recently visited the parish church of Castleton in the Peak District and discovered that the vicar of Castleton was living in Hope!

12 April

A mill owner decided to send his son to a public school. The lad spoke with a broad Yorkshire accent and so it was arranged that he would live with the local rector and his family so as to improve his English. A few months later the boy's father called at the rectory to see how his son was getting on. The door was answered by the rector who greeted him with the words, "Lad, am I glad to see thee."

22 September

Some boys stopped to collect conkers on the way to church. As a result they were late and they entered the church just as the congregation were singing the first hymn:

See the conquering heroes come.

Our minister says

Happiness is like jam: you can't spread even a little without getting some on yourself.

21 September

Notice outside a Methodist Church

TIRED OUT AND RUN DOWN?
COME IN FOR A SERVICE

Sorry rector

One Sunday after an illness that had left me temporarily deaf, I happened to say to one of my office-bearers, "That was a strange experience, I could not hear myself preach."

"My," he said, "you were lucky."

20 September

Whilst another tombstone has
these words:

HERE LIES ANN MANN
SHE LIVED AN OLD MAID
AND DIED AN OLD MANN

15 April

From America

When I was on the diocesan staff and after retirement, I was a frequent visitor to the parish of St Michael and All Angels in Anniston, Alabama. Upon one of my Sunday visits I was to have been welcomed in the Sunday bulletin with the comment: "Dr Gribben has been with us frequently." A typing error caused my presence to be acknowledged with: "Dr Gribben has beer with us frequently."

E.G. in Episcopal Life

19 September

On another tombstone are the words:

HERE LIES ONE WOOD,
ENCLOSED IN WOOD
ONE WOOD WITHIN
THE OTHER,
THE OUTER WOOD WAS
VERY GOOD –
WE CANNOT PRAISE
THE OTHER.

16 April

On the gates of the Winnipeg Anglican
Cathedral which is situated in a
cemetery, appear two notices:

THE ANGLICAN CHURCH
WELCOMES YOU

THE PREMISES ARE PROTECTED
BY GUARD DOGS

The Anglican Digest

Some epitaphs

Seen on a dentist's tombstone:

STRANGER APPROACH THE
GROUND WITH GRAVITY
JOHN BROWN IS FILLING
HIS FINAL CAVITY

A man had the following inscription put on his wife's tombstone:

THE LIGHT OF MY LIFE HAS GONE OUT

Some years later after he had remarried someone had written underneath:

NOW HE HAS STRUCK ANOTHER MATCH

17 September

Grave situations

The rector announced, "I am sure that you will not wish to overwork our visiting priest while I am on holiday, and will keep funerals to a minimum."

18 April

When her husband was near to death his wife ordered a headstone and asked that REST IN PEACE be carved on it. This was done but after the man died and the will was read, his widow found that he had left the bulk of his fortune elsewhere. So she told the stonemason to add:

TILL I COME

16 September

A wedding at our small village church was quite an occasion. However, when people started to find the first hymn on the hymn board they realized that something was wrong:

Hymn 413 "Rejoice for a brother deceased" should, of course, have been Hymn 431 "Love divine all loves excelling".

19 April

The *Accrington Observer* reported the
retirement of Joe Burns, superintendent
at the local crematorium. "Joe, 60, was
presented with a barbecue set."

Daily Telegraph

A rector was doing some parish visiting and called on one of his parishioners. During the course of their conversation he remarked that he hadn't seen her in church recently. "No," came the reply, "my daughter is learning to play the harp and I'm having second thoughts about going to heaven."

20 April

From the U.S.A.

The rector of a church in Washington DC had just made the happy announcement that a member of the congregation was with child. Then he reminisced a bit: "There were no pregnancies in this parish until I arrived," he beamed.

14 September

In the course of his sermon the minister asked anyone who had not sinned to stand up. To his amazement an elderly gentleman stood up immediately. "Are you sure you've never sinned?" the minister asked.

"Oh yes, I've sinned," he replied, "I'm standing on behalf of my wife's first husband."

21 April

Gorgeous

At one time my husband, George, a priest in the Episcopal Church, did an interim in Texas assisting a bishop. When it came time to line up for the recessional, the acolyte (a young boy) came up to George, who was wearing his red chimere rochet and Indian beaded stole, and said in a whisper, "Just love your outfit."

PSST. YOU MUST GIVE THE NAME OF YOUR TAILOR...

13 September

Canon Douglas Feaver (later Bishop of Peterborough) once conducted a service at our club for the hard of hearing. When my husband told him, "I am a Methodist," he quickly (and typically) replied, "That can easily be rectified!"

22 April

Our lady doctor took her very small niece to church. When they returned her mother asked the little girl what happened.

"Well, the minister prayed and I prayed. The minister sang and I sang. The minister speaked and Auntie brought me home."

12 September

One Sunday the minister announced that the Young Wives were staging a new display in the vestry hall. After the service an elderly gentleman said,

"What's this about a NUDIST PLAY?"

23 April

Mower power

During a stewardship campaign in a small village in Northamptonshire one parishioner covenanted his promised giving and added a pledge:

To keep God's mower a cut above the rest.

11 September

*A small boy, seeing a funeral procession going **up** the street, asked his mother what it was. She told him: "It's someone who has died on their way to heaven." Some time later the little lad saw a similar procession coming **down** the street. He said, "Hard luck on that one, Mum!"*

24 April

The village parson was dragging through his sermon when he observed that the congregation had fallen asleep, except the local idiot sitting at the back. "What's this," he roared, "everyone asleep but this poor simpleton?"

Came a voice from the back, "Aye, and if I wasn't so simple, I should be asleep an' all."

10 September

Nearing the end

A lay preacher caused much amusement by sometimes using words in the wrong context. Towards the end of a very long sermon he remarked, "Just a few more words and then I will decease."

Two young tourists went into a Quaker guest house in the Lakeland. As they were strangers the warden approached and asked, "Are you Friends?"

Back came the reply "No, we're married."

The rector was on a railway station with a party of children.

A porter came up to him and said, "Excuse me, are you St Michael and the Angels?"

26 April

During an Advent *Songs of Praise* from Northampton the presenter opened the programme from the top of the Express Lift Tower. After his introduction he started going down the steps as he announced the first hymn:

Lo, He comes with clouds descending

8 September

True story

Whilst on holiday in Stornoway, we attended morning service at St Peter's Episcopal Church. The minister had given the final blessing and together with the visiting preacher and two servers filed towards the vestry, which is situated at the front of the church. To the words of the hymn "No door shall keep him out" the minister vainly tried to open the vestry door. Fortunately a watchful sidesman, realizing there was a problem, came to the rescue with a spare key, and the moment became a holiday memory.

27 April

A little girl was stationed at the church door to await the arrival of her rather large aunt who was attending the harvest festival. Her aunt was a little late arriving and they entered the church together just as the congregation were singing:

All things bright and beautiful
All creatures great and small

Really!

The church bulletin advertising a concert said:

Tickets include a glass of wine and a nibble from the rector.

I'M SURE SOMETHING'S JUST BITTEN ME!

28 April

A very small woman was the visiting preacher at a church in Scotland. After a few minutes she called, "Can you hear me at the back?"

A voice replied, "We can hear you, hen. We just canna see you."

6 September

A woman was sending an old family bible through the post. As the parcel was being weighed at the post office she was asked, "Does it contain any breakables?"

"Well, no," she replied, "nothing except the ten commandments."

29 April

A member of the Free Church of Scotland gave the minister a bottle of cherry brandy on the understanding that it would be acknowledged in the church magazine. In the next edition the minister thanked Mrs Mackintosh for the gift of cherries and the spirit in which it was given.

5 September

The minister was very depressed when he arrived back home from the doctor's. "What's the matter, dear?" asked his wife.

"Well," said the minister, "the doctor's told me that I've got to take these pills for the rest of my life."

"That's not so bad, is it?" said his wife cheerfully. "It is," replied the minister. "He's only given me seven pills."

30 April

The young curate didn't get on too well with his rather pompous rector. In due course he was appointed to another church and for his last sermon in the parish he chose as his text:

"Tarry ye here with the ass while I go yonder."

4 September

This and that

A former Bishop of Exeter was rather absent-minded. One day he went by train to take a confirmation service in a neighbouring town. When the ticket collector asked to see his ticket he couldn't find it. The kindly ticket collector said, "Don't worry, My Lord, I know who you are." The bishop replied, "But I do worry because without the ticket I don't know where I'm going."

OH MR PORTER, WHAT SHALL I DO?!

1 May

The same rector went on holiday to Jerusalem where, to the surprise of his flock, he met the woman of his choice. News of his forthcoming marriage soon reached the parish and the following Sunday the organist marked the event by playing the voluntary "Pray for the peace of Jerusalem".

You – me – and us

*An old woman, who was very often **the** congregation of a tiny West Country church, was asked how they managed.*

"Oh, we're fine," was her confident reply. "Rector does the 'God be-ses', and I do the 'As it wases'."

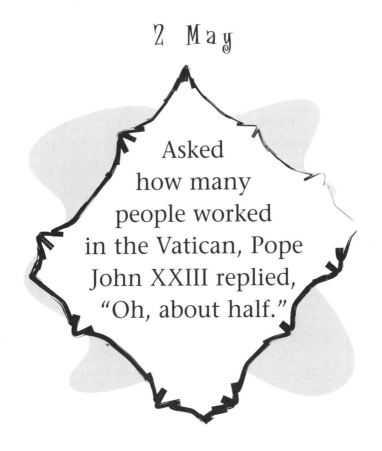

2 May

Asked how many people worked in the Vatican, Pope John XXIII replied, "Oh, about half."

2 September

Comfort and joy

At a theological college in Canada, the students often went to take services at mission churches in the neighbouring countryside. One student, whose surname was Joy, overstayed his absence. When he received a message from the college warden expressing his disapproval, the student sent the following reply:

See Psalm 30 verse 5 [KJV]

which reads: "Weeping may endure for a night, but JOY cometh in the morning."

3 May

A bishop speaking about the "Water of Life" asked the younger members of the congregation where their drinking water came from. A little boy jumped up and quickly said,

"From the Lord my pump."

1 September

The minister and his wife had been on a safari holiday and upon their return showed their slides to the Church Guild. At the end of the evening a rather ageing deacon got up and gave a vote of thanks. He closed with a prayer.

*Dear everlasting Lord, we thank you that our minister and his wife are safely back from holiday. And we thank you Lord for **man and his beast**.*

4 May

A Methodist minister was stopped in the High Street one Saturday morning by a Salvation Army lassie who asked: "Are you saved?" He replied with a smile, "My dear, I'm a Methodist minister."

"Don't let that make any difference," she replied.

31 August

Methodist ministers sometimes take it into their heads to dress up as John Wesley. One such minister dressed himself suitably and rode through the streets of his town, stopping at the market place where he delivered a short homily seated on his horse. One young man was heard to say to his girlfriend, "Now I know what is meant by the **Sermon on the Mount**."

5 May

It really happened

At our Methodist church the minister announced, "We'll now sing 'Stand up, stand up for Jesus' and we'll sing this one sitting down."

30 August

One day
I was visiting
the maternity ward
at our local hospital. I
asked one of the women if she
had been confirmed. She
replied, "What do you
think I am here
now for?"

6 May

Spoonerisms

W. A. Spooner, an Anglican clergyman, was at one time warden of New College, Oxford. A nervous man, he had difficulty in getting his words out, resulting in numerous verbal blunders, to the delight of the undergraduates, who undoubtedly added to the range.

He became famous for telling an absent youth that:

You have hissed my mystery lesson.

29 August

When I became choirmaster at a
small mission church I inherited two
ancient choirmen who had been
taught to bellow from an early age.
It was their opinion that the louder
the singing, the better the service
and they translated

pp to mean "plenty of power"
and FF to mean "FULL FORCE".

7 May

Whilst conducting worship in the chapel of New College, Oxford he announced the first line of a hymn as:

Kingquering congs their titles take.

A new young minister would ask the prospective bride and groom if they attended church. Relating this to a friend the next day, the bride-to-be said, "I told him we go to church every Sunday on television."

8 May

Some years ago various original ecclesiastical Spoonerisms were published in the *Church Times*. Two have remained in my mind:

TELL ME, DEAR - ARE YOU A CROOK OR A NANNY?

The vicar knows every crook and nanny in the parish

Here comes the rector, fight the liar

27 August

A woman patient arrived rather late for our morning service at the hospital chapel. She later apologised to the chaplain explaining that she had had to go back to the ward to get her hat so that she was properly dressed. The chaplain smilingly wondered when she had last attended church in her nightie, dressing gown and hat!

9 May

A real pain

A clergyman was standing in for a rector who was ill. The parish was in a very rough part, most of the windows had been broken and were boarded up with cardboard. On his last Sunday he told the congregation, "I have enjoyed being with you but of course I am not your rector, rather like those pieces of cardboard in your windows – they're not real panes, they are a substitute, and I have been a substitute." At the end of the service the church warden thanked him for helping and said, "We want you to know, sir, that you have not been a substitute, you have been a real pain."

26 August

One Sunday morning after Communion the congregation were having refreshments in the hall. I was chatting to the parents of a toddler who was tearing around, very interested in everything. "He's a live wire," I commented. "Oh yes," was the reply. "The other day we had friends in for sherry and asked him to take crisps round. When we next saw him he was approaching each person with the container, pausing and solemnly taking a crisp out, handing it to the guest with the words: 'The Body of Christ'."

10 May

The rector had his bike stolen. The police duly recovered it and the overjoyed cleric immediately pedalled down to his church to thank God for its recovery. He went in to pray. When he came out it had gone again.

25 August

True stories

I have recently been appointed electoral roll officer at our church. One of the women will insist on calling it the electrical roll. She probably imagines that you have to be a bright spark to be put on it.

11 May

Keep smiling – and if you meet someone without a smile give them one of yours.

24 August

One of our preachers was very small of stature and when he sat down in the pulpit during the hymn before the sermon he was completely out of sight. One Sunday we finished the hymn and sat patiently waiting for him to appear. Several minutes passed and we wondered if he had dozed off when he suddenly reappeared and announced his text:

IT IS I – BE NOT AFRAID.

12 May

A minister, on visiting his local hospital, would glance at the list of patients on display in the sister's office. He noticed that the letters R.C. appeared frequently after the names of patients and remarked one day to the sister on the high percentage of Roman Catholics. "Oh, that's not their denomination," replied the sister smiling, "R.C. stands for their breakfast preference – rice crispies."

23 August

The clerk of the local district council thought he would take the rise out of the local rector who had reported that some gypsies had deposited a dead donkey at the gate of the church. The clerk wrote that it was surely the rector's job to bury the dead. The rector replied politely that it was his first duty to consult the relatives.

13 May

Advice from Dr Spurgeon to trainee ministers about to preach their first sermons

"When you speak of heaven, let your face light up with a heavenly glow. Let your eyes shine with reflected glory. But when you speak of hell your ordinary face will do."

22 August

A farmer was reading the word at morning service. As he reached the bottom of the page, he read the words "and Moses was sick". He then turned over two pages at once, and continued "and the lot fell on Aaron".

14 May

Before suggesting a new convert should embrace the Roman Catholic faith, the priest thought he ought to test her opinion about divorce. "If your husband ever left you, would you consider marrying again?" he began.

"No, thank you," she replied, "but it was nice of you to ask."

A child was asked why no man can serve two masters. He promptly replied, "Because you are not allowed to have two wives."

15 May

A Mr Smith and a Revd Smith lived in the same street. Mr Smith had left on a visit to India when his clergyman neighbour died. On arrival in India Mr Smith sent a cable to his wife, but, unfortunately, by mistake it was delivered to the Revd Smith's widow. She, no doubt, was surprised when she read, "Arrived safely – heat terrific."

20 August

Holy smoke

A six-year-old girl making her first visit to St Thomas's, Hereford, Texas, said to her father afterwards, "They tried to run us out – they brought a smoke bomb and shook it at the people in the front row, but we didn't leave. We stayed there until the end."

16 May

The parish newsletter reported that the curate would be celebrating for the next fortnight whilst the rector was on holiday.

———— ⧫⧫⧫ ————

19 August

The notice read

The women of the church have cast off clothing of every kind and they can be seen in the basement of the church on Friday afternoon

17 May

From this day forward

A quiet wedding had taken place at a church, which was part of a multi-purpose building. Everybody had gone into the vestry for the signing of the registers, when in came the young man who was running the evening disco and he had a new tape that he wanted to try out. Just as he put it on, the wedding party emerged from the vestry to the strains of: "On the baby's knuckle or the baby's knee, where will the baby's dimple be?"

18 August

The parish newsletter at Long Ditton, Surrey announced:

Prayers for peace this month have been cancelled because of the new rector coming to St Christopher's.

18 May

The woman organist at a village church had just been jilted after a fairly long engagement to a local preacher. About a fortnight after this outwardly unhappy event he was due to preach at her church. She was seated at the organ immediately below him and facing the pulpit when he announced his text – 1 Samuel 28:7.

Seek me a woman [ESV]

17 August

On another occasion, after he had given the address at a wedding in a northern cathedral, the organist complimented him with the words, "Thank you for your sermon. We always like having visiting preachers. It helps us to appreciate our own clergy all the more"!

19 May

Said the rector at a wedding:

"Don't be nervous for, you see,
Everything that's said and done,
You say or do it after me."

"Wilt thou take and wed this woman
And endeavour to be true?"
But the bridegroom, much
embarrassed,
Only stammered: "After you"!

16 August

True story

Some years ago when Archdeacon George Austin was the visiting preacher at a public school he was introduced by a pupil who then announced the theme for the Sunday: "We welcome today Canon George Austin – God has chosen the weak things of the world to confound the wisdom of the mighty."

20 May

Signing the register at a wedding, the best man had difficulty in making his ballpoint pen work. "Put your weight on it," said the vicar. He duly signed:

John Smith (ten stone four pounds).

15 August

The minister had no knowledge of the deceased and in fact realized to his horror as he entered the pulpit that he was uncertain of the sex. "We meet today to pay tribute to our dear departed er … " – leaning over to a relative he whispered, "Brother or sister?" Back came the reply, "Cousin."

Did you hear of the bride who wanted to make sure that she did the right thing when entering the church on her wedding day? She kept saying to herself, "Aisle; altar; hymn": "I'll alter him."

14 August

The chaplain was visiting a patient who was in hospital for a minor operation. After a chat he said, "Perhaps you would like to come to the service on Sunday morning – that is – if you are still with us?"

22 May

Arriving at church
to attend a wedding,
a woman in a large hat
was tackled by the usher.
"Are you a friend of the
groom?"

"Certainly not," she
replied, "I'm the bride's
mother."

A former Bishop of Guildford, while in civilian dress, was invited by a woman to hear her daughter in a concert at Guildford Cathedral. She asked the bishop if he knew where the cathedral was. "Yes," said the bishop, "I have a part-time Sunday job there."

23 May

A young curate had been far too popular with the women of the parish and was causing much embarrassment to all concerned. Eventually the Rector had to ask him to leave and find another place to practise his ministry. "I don't know why you are so worried, Rector," he said. "After all, there's safety in numbers."

"That's where you're wrong," replied the Rector. "Your only safety is in Exodus."

12 August

A bishop invited all his junior clergy to join him at an unknown destination for a clergy refresher course. When the train finally stopped they were surprised to see that they had arrived at Dymchurch. One curate was heard to remark, "He could have chosen a more appropriate venue."

24 May

A young nurse who had been attending church for a few months was leaving to go to another hospital. The minister said, "We are sorry that Mary is leaving us; some nurses have long stays, and others have short stays."

11 August

True story

A former Bishop of Guildford told the story of an ACCM selection conference held at his home for those hoping to be accepted for training for the ministry. The young men were told not to leave the grounds. The bishop had to go to Guildford and suddenly came face to face with one of the candidates who looked flustered and said, "The Holy Spirit told me I must come shopping."

"Oh dear," said the bishop, "one of you must be wrong, it's early closing day."

25 May

A U.R.C. minister was showing his two grandsons around the parish church. There happened to be a knight and his lady in two separate vaults, one over the other. The boys were at different ends of the church when one shouted to the other: "Come and see what I've found – BUNK BEDS!"

10 August

Burnt offering

Scouts, Guides and Brownies joined our congregation for our Candlemass service. As each person lit their candle and joined in the procession around the church, one Brownie was quite oblivious of the actions of the Cub Scout behind her. As she joyfully sang "Jesus bids us shine" he held his candle rather close to her long hair and the smell of burning hair soon filled the building.

26 May

Headline in a local paper

*PENSIONERS WED –
Fifty years friendship
ends at altar.*

9 August

When (in 1958)
Bishop Roger Wilson asked
for his personal mail to be
forwarded, he said that his new
address would be The Palace,
Chichester. The girl asked
him, "Would that be
a dance hall or
a cinema?"

Another interesting wedding announcement was when Mr Savage married Miss Wild.

8 August

Whilst the service was in progress at our village chapel a combine harvester was cutting an adjoining field of wheat. Suddenly smoke billowed past the windows and we learnt that the combine had caught fire, burnt out and set fire to the field of corn. Meanwhile we in the chapel were singing the hymn "O thou who camest from above" which includes the words: "There let it for thy glory burn with inextinguishable blaze."

28 May

A rather eccentric incumbent always had to be known as "Rector". He regarded it almost as an insult if he was addressed in any other way. He went to great pains to explain this when he came into school to take the assembly. Hopeful that he had got his point across, he finished:

Now you don't call me mister,
You don't call me sir,
You don't call me vicar,
What do you call me?

A shattering reply from a little boy at the back of the hall:

My dad says you're a silly old man.

7 August

True stories

An elderly steward in Yorkshire welcomed the woman lay preacher with the words,

"Well, come on, lass, let's have you in the pulpit. Sooner you're in, sooner you're out, and sooner we get home to the Yorkshire pudding."

29 May

Thank you, Lord, for giving us the ability to laugh at ourselves ... to all who have received, **Pass this gift on to others**.

A teacher asked young William, "Do you pray at home before meals?"

Back came the reply, "We don't need to Miss, my mother's a good cook."

30 May

From the notices

We are pleased to report that the Young People's Group and the Mothers' Union are all growing in size.

5 August

A little boy said to his mother after saying his bedtime prayers, "Do we pray to God at night to get the cheap rate?"

31 May

Some years ago the bishop was visiting an outlying parish and the rector decided it would be a good idea to take him on his rounds in his pony and trap. Unfortunately while struggling to pull his weighty burden up a steep hill the pony noisily passed wind. The rector, somewhat embarrassed, apologized. The bishop replied, "Oh that's all right, I didn't realize it was you, I thought it was your pony."

4 August

An honest seven year old admitted calmly that Bobby Smith had kissed her after Sunday School. "How did it happen?" her mother gasped.

"It wasn't easy," came the reply, "three girls helped me to catch him."

1 June

On his way to a funeral the minister leaned forward and tapped the driver on the shoulder to ask him a question. When the driver visibly jumped, the minister apologized for startling him. "That's all right, sir," the driver replied. "It's just that I usually drive the hearse."

A Sunday School teacher asked the children, "Why is it necessary to be quiet in church?" A little girl replied, "Because people are sleeping."

2 June

During a holiday at the seaside our small son discovered the slot machines in a nearby amusement arcade. Shortly after returning home we visited a neighbouring church for the flower festival. When we passed the slots in the wall for magazine monies etc. he said in a loud voice, "What do you get out of those money slots, Daddy?"

2 August

An elder sister was explaining to her young brother how wrong it was to work on Sundays. "But policemen work on Sundays, don't they go to heaven?" he wanted to know. "No," said his sister, "they're not needed up there."

3 June

At a meeting of the Women's Bright Hour an elderly member told everyone to boycott the new launderette after she had seen a notice above the machines:

WHEN THE LIGHT GOES OUT, PLEASE REMOVE ALL YOUR CLOTHES

A minister had a notice put on the church notice board:

IF YOU ARE TIRED OF SIN COME IN

Underneath someone had written:

IF NOT, PHONE 264 45168

4 June

My daughter, aged eight, attended the parish Communion. She watched the bread and wine being prepared with great interest. When the congregation left their seats to receive the sacrament she whispered: "Do you think it would be all right if I joined in with the commotion?"

SUNDAY SERVICES

9.30am Matins
10.30am Holy Commotion
6.30pm Evensong

31 July

Once at an open air meeting I was asked the question: "What is the shape of the soul after death?" I replied, "Oblong."

5 June

From the October parish magazine

Most of the church activities have resumed after the summer break. The Ladies' Choir have started rehearsals and we expect the Rifle Club to be in action before long.

To commemorate the Feast of St Francis the children brought their pets to church – hamsters, gerbils, rabbits etc. As the rector settled everyone ready for a prayer, a pony was ridden rather noisily up the marble aisle. Stopping nose to nose with the rector, the young equestrian fought to turn the pony round. The manoeuvre was finally accomplished as we reached the part when we all say, "We have left undone those things which we ought to have done." Then as we reached the words "And have done those things which we ought NOT to have done," the pony **did**.

6 June

Magazine quote

As many of you know, the fire last week at our sister church was put out by the prompt action of the Ladies' Circle, who quickly turned themselves into a bucket chain. A special mention must go to Mrs Treeves-Jones who spent two hours passing water.

29 July

At the annual church bazaar, our family gave a Siamese kitten for a "Guess the Name" competition. Being black and white, it was called "Whisky". When the winner was announced, a deaf lady at the back of the hall said,

"Disgraceful, Mrs. MacFarlane winning whisky at a church event."

7 June

A notice in the church newsletter said:

Would the person who took the step ladder yesterday please return it or further steps will be taken.

28 July

True stories

Bishop David Sheppard, former England cricketer, shares the following true story about his wife Grace, who was a governor of a comprehensive school. On one occasion when the governors were interviewing for the appointment of a deputy head, the chairman of the governors introduced her with the words,

"This is Mrs Bishop, the wife of the famous footballer."

8 June

I HEARD THE VOICE
OF JESUS SAY

The collection will
be taken during this
hymn.

27 July

From the mission field

The sacristan was so pleased to inform the congregation that their priest had recovered from his illness. He displayed the following notice:

God is good.
The priest is better.

9 June

From a Scout carol service sheet

Hail the heaven born
price of peace
Hail the sin of
righteousness

26 July

Another church notice board said:

DANGER LIVE CHURCH!

10 June

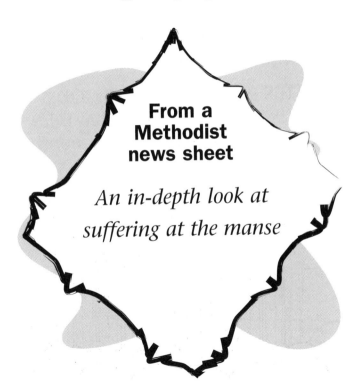

From a Methodist news sheet

An in-depth look at suffering at the manse

25 July

A notice on a church door in Cheshire

THIS IS THE HOUSE OF GOD.
THIS IS THE GATE OF HEAVEN.
(This door is locked in winter months)

11 June

From Worcester

The church fabric officer reported that the need for a toilet was identified more than 30 years ago, but the cost and the construction difficulties blocked it.

24 July

Whilst a dual purpose notice board giving details of the following Sunday's service had:

SERMON
WHY DIVORCE?

ANTHEM
I SAW ANOTHER ANGEL

12 June

Another parish bulletin reported

Eileen Jones remains in hospital and needs blood donors for more transfusions. She is also having trouble sleeping and requests tapes of the minister's sermons.

23 July

Another text:

WHAT IS HELL LIKE?

was accompanied by:

COME AND HEAR OUR CHOIR

13 June

A letter from a schoolboy at a preparatory school to his parents

Dear Mum,
    Last week the bishop came for confirmation. I could see him well from the seat in the chapel. Now I know what a crook really looks like.

22 July

You must have seen the dual purpose notice boards with a section for a wayside pulpit text, and another section for service details etc. Sometimes they make interesting reading. One read:

The Lord Bishop will be here next Sunday at 6.30 p.m.

on the other side were the words

DON'T WORRY, IT MAY NEVER HAPPEN

14 June

On leaving an interdenominational lunch the Catholic priest was heard to say to the Methodist minister, "Well, we're all doing the Lord's work – you in your way and I in His."

21 July

Whilst the message on another
notice board was:

**Come and talk to the listening God
You can bank on him.**

15 June

At a Methodist church a certain woman who was nearly always late for the service arrived as the congregation started to sing:

With early feet I love to appear among the saints.

20 July

The notice outside our local church said:

**We are at your service
Why not come to ours?**

16 June

The restoration of the church was finally completed by the resurfacing of the driveway. The following Sunday the secretary praised everyone who had helped and gave special thanks to the minister and his wife who had rolled in the new gravel.

19 July

Notice on a door in Istanbul

American Dentist –
2nd Floor.
Teeth extracted by
new Methodist.

A reader taking his first service asked his rector what he should preach about. The rector replied, "Ten minutes and God."

18 July

Seen on a church notice board

CARPENTER
NEEDS JOINERS

18 June

During the Second World War, parts of Birmingham suffered severe bombing. One morning after a particularly bad night only a few teachers and children gathered in the school assembly hall. The headmaster asked if anyone had a favourite hymn. A small boy's hand shot up. "Please can we have 'Glad that I live am I'?"

17 July

Seen in a Connecticut church bulletin

Tuesday at 4 p.m. there will be an Ice Cream Social.

All women giving milk please come early.

19 June

Parson thoughts

A passenger plane flew into a severe storm. As the passengers were being bounced about by the turbulence, a young woman turned to the minister sitting next to her and nervously asked, "Reverend, you're a man of God, can't you do something about this storm?"

He replied, "Madam, I'm in sales not management."

16 July

The minister announced that the sermon on Sunday would be shorter than usual – five minutes at the most. The choir then rendered the anthem "It is enough".

20 June

The new rector remarked to his churchwarden, "Have you noticed that after the service several of the men go over to the local inn?"

"Oh, yes," replied the warden. "I think it's their thirst after righteousness."

15 July

From the notices

During the clergy conference a skeleton staff will be left in each deanery for cemetery duty.

21 June

The rector said to a young woman parishioner, "You know I pray for you every night."

She replied: "I'm afraid it's too late, rector, I'm engaged to be married."

14 July

Seen on a church notice board

Unlike the post office we have two collections every Sunday

22 June

One Sunday the priest told his congregation that he had good news and bad news. He proceeded to tell them the bad news that the church urgently needed £2,000 to repair the roof. The congregation groaned. He cut them short by telling them the good news. There was enough money to cover the repairs. The congregation breathed a sigh of relief. "The final piece of bad news," said the priest, "is that the money is still in your pockets."

13 July

Notice in a train window

RESERVED FOR BARE METHODISTS

(It appears that Methodists from Bare were spending a day at the seaside long before topless bathing was allowed.)

23 June

From Ireland

The village church was packed for Sunday Mass when three strangers entered. The priest, spotting them, said, "Three chairs for the visitors."

The congregation quickly responded with: "Hip, Hip, Hooray."

12 July

**Seen on a church notice board
in Cornwall**

Morning Service
11 a.m.   Mr Philpot

Evening Service
6.30 p.m.   Mr Spilit

24 June

Wrong number

The curate took his wife to the maternity hospital and said that he would ring later for news. When he phoned later in the day he called the wrong number and got the county cricket ground. He said, "I brought my wife to your place this morning, is there any news?" He was surprised to be told, "Yes, there are nine out and the last two were ducks."

11 July

Notice in a church hall where a sale of second-hand clothes was in progress

Women may have a fit upstairs

25 June

Even church councils have their
funny side.

The minutes of one P.C.C. read:
"The money raised from the
MUMBLE SALE will go towards the
vestry carpet. The rector said that he
would converse with the treasurer."

At another meeting one old
gentleman, when asked to cast
his vote, said, **"I recline."** Come
to think of it the meeting had
gone on for a bit.

10 July

From the U.S.A.

Notice outside a New York
convalescent home:

For the sick and tired
of the Episcopal
Church

26 June

Our church council, who had a reputation for putting every important item off until the next meeting, were discussing a Free Will Offering Scheme. The rector, anxious to get home to his television set, closed the meeting with the words: "So it's unanimous then. We make the Free Will Offering compulsory."

9 July

From the notices

Church advertising for a new rector:

Wages not high, but retirement benefits out of this world

27 June

**Notice outside a
north London church**

WANTED – WORKERS FOR GOD – PLENTY OF OVERTIME

8 July

A little boy was pulling a terrible face in Sunday School. His teacher said: "Bobby, when I was a little girl I was told that if I pulled a face like that it would freeze and stay like it."

The boy looked at her and replied, "Well Miss, you can't say that you weren't warned."

28 June

Good for nothing

Two young women were discussing their future husbands. One said, "I'm going to marry a doctor, then I can be ill for nothing." The other replied, "I'll marry a minister, then I can be good for nothing."

7 July

A young boy discovered a Bible in the attic, opened it and found a large leaf pressed between the pages of Genesis. "Oh, look," he said, "Adam's left his clothes here."

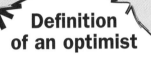

**Definition
of an optimist**

*A woman who slips her
feet back into her shoes
when the minister says,
"And finally …"*

6 July

Paul had been a good boy, so his mum gave him 50p to go and buy some sweets. However he didn't say "Thank you", so she said, "Paul, have you forgotten something? What do I say to Daddy when he gives me money?"

"Is that all?" replied Paul innocently.

Well, she did ask.

30 June

The rector was taking the funeral of
one of his congregation.

At the graveside after the committal,
he tried to console and comfort the widow.
The rector asked, "What happened to
your husband?"

The widow said, "Well, rector, I was
cutting up a cabbage for dinner when
he died suddenly by my side." "Oh dear,"
said the rector, "what did you do?"

"Well," she said, "I had to open
a tin of peas."

5 July

Philip and John were being put to bed by their grandmother who had come to stay for Christmas. They had had their baths and were saying their prayers while Gran tidied up the bathroom. John, the younger lad, finished his prayers with a list of things he wanted for Christmas, saying them at the top of his voice.

"Quiet!" Philip said, "God isn't deaf."

"No," said John, "but Gran is."

1 July

Revd Samuel Jordan had a son at college preparing to take his final examinations. He asked him to be sure to let him know how he got on. One day the rector received an e-mail which read, "Hymn 179, verse 5, last line". Looking up the hymn in the hymn book, he was pleased to read,

**Sorrow vanquished,
labour ended,
Jordan passed.**

4 July

A Sunday School teacher asked her class to write a list of eleven great men. As they were busy writing she walked between the tables and noticed one little lad chewing the end of his pen. "Have you finished?" she asked.

"Not quite, Miss," came the reply. "I'm trying to decide on the goalkeeper."

2 July

It was the minister's first Sunday after his induction.

The steward giving out the notices said, "I am sorry to say that we have dry rot in the pews and floor, and as you can see we have got the worm in the pulpit."

3 July

Revd Edwin Softly was the special
preacher at a chapel service.
The woman conducting the service
gave out the hymn before the sermon,
which was "Tell me the old old story".
She then read the verse:

Tell me the story SOFTLY
With earnest tones and grave,
Remember I'm the sinner,
Whom Jesus came to save!